The Long Distance Romance Guide

The Long Distance Romance Guide

A Handbook of Encouragement to Help You Stay Close When Apart

Leslie Karsner
Romance Coach
Founder, RomanceInstitute.com

Writers Club Press
San Jose New York Lincoln Shanghai

The Long Distance Romance Guide
A Handbook of Encouragement
to Help You Stay Close When Apart
All Rights Reserved © 2001 by Leslie Waugh Karsner

Writers Club Press
an imprint of iUniverse.com, Inc.

For information address:
iUniverse.com, Inc.
5220 S 16th, Ste. 200
Lincoln, NE 68512
www.iuniverse.com

ISBN: 0-595-09181-4

Printed in the United States of America

If the dull substance of my flesh were thought,
Injurious distance should not stop my way;
For then despite of space I would be brought,
From limits far remote where thou dost stay.
No matter then although my foot did stand
Upon the farthest earth removed from thee;
For nimble thought can jump both sea and land
As soon as think the place where he would be.

from Sonnet XLIV by William Shakespeare

CONTENTS

APPRECIATION

In coaching people to have a romance with life, I often find that those who seem to have it all have a hard time appreciating it. Some of my most successful clients come to me because they can't remember the last time they reacted—to anything—by tingling, glowing, blushing, swooning, getting goosebumps or feeling butterflies in their stomach.

These are some of the physical responses we experience when we really appreciate something. And having just completed this Guide, I'm simply *reeling* with appreciation from all the help I received!

My big brother collaborated with me on this book even though he didn't want any credit. His own experience in LDRs, along with a Master's Degree from NYU in Interactive Telecommunications, proved invaluable in making this Guide complete and definitive. Together we co-founded *RomanceInstitute.com*. Thank you, Jeff!

This book would not exist were it not for my wonderful coaching clients who make long-distance romance work every day. I'm blessed to work with such hearty romantics. I thank them for sharing their secrets with me for this Guide…it's dedicated to you!

Finally, I'd be remiss if I didn't acknowlege my own LDRs. Here's a wink and a few long-distance "air kisses" to past boyfriends who managed the distance in order to share my heart, beginning in my college years and extending through to my recent history. It's with them that I first began developing the principles of distance mangement for romance.

If you appreciate what we've done here, if we help you bring goosebumps to your far-off lover, or if you have anything to add which might help others in LDRs, please let me know at our web site, *RomanceInstitute.com*. If we all put our heads together, the LDR community need no longer be underserved.

I hope you and your lover will appreciate the delights to be found in the following pages. That means savor, blush, swoon…

INTRODUCTION

So you're in love! How wonderful!! You must be so very—

What's that?! Your lover's away so you sit around pining? Then you call each other to whine about the pining? She misses him more…no, he misses her more…*miss schmiss!!*

I've been in a few long-term long distance romances (LDRs) myself, and let me share one observation with you right from the start: missing your lover is *zero-benefit torment!* It's fruitless frustration. You never feel any better after putting yourself through it. After all, missing someone involves idealizing the past and future…but what about the present? This Guide is your present!

The LDR Guide will help make your absent lover seem more present through better distance management. You'll learn secrets to help you approach the time apart as extended foreplay. Even though your lover happens to live far away or travel a lot, by utilizing this Guide you will soon find yourself enjoying and celebrating your relationship every day!

Living your lives apart doesn't mean your life is missing anything. And it doesn't mean that you live your relationship in stops (time apart) and starts (time together.) Just as lovers who are present can seem absent, those who are absent can be made to seem present. I'll show you how!

"Absence diminishes mediocre passions and increases great ones, as the wind blows out candles and fans fires."
Francois, Duc de La Rochefoucauld

As a Romance Coach, I've coached dozens and interviewed hundreds of people in long-distance romances (LDRs). I've witnessed my own friends and clients spend too many days, weeks and months missing absent lovers—and not doing anything about it!

True love is the only reason to go through an LDR. If the love is true, the distance can be managed.

Trying to "get to know" someone far away through occasional visits is a tall order. It's asking a lot of someone you just met to enter into an LDR with you. But when two people decide to "go the distance" in an LDR, it signifies that both regard this as a relationship that matters.

You'll note throughout the book that I say "romance" instead of "relationship". That's because I'm writing this for everyone from those who've just met (who might not yet call their romance a relationship) to those who've been married for years (who might need reminding that their relationship *should* be a romance!) And I do refer to those involved as "lovers"—even though they might not yet be in love or have proclaimed it.

I write about romance, not relationship counselling. If you're having issues with your relationship, I'd suggest you see a counselor. Like I tell my clients, "I can't fan the fires if the wood is green!" This book is written for those who are off and running in a romance that is healthy enough to flourish locally…but you simply find yourself, for the time being, geographically challenged.

"Some people believe that keeping up a long-distance romance is like trying to ride a bicycle through the snow: a doomed, wobbily enterprise."
Wedding Section, New York Times

I know firsthand what you're up against. Friends may say it'll never last ("Out of sight, out of mind!") Family members encourage you to find someone local. But all you ought to do is simply listen to your heart and read this Guide.

Distance needn't put your romance in a cryogenic state—read on if you want to stop putting your love life on hold and actually move it along. You don't need to relate to your lover with bursts of togetherness only when you're under the same roof.

Just because you're in different locations doesn't mean you can't experience most of the vitality, passion, magic and comfort of a close-proximity romance. Distance doesn't destroy romance, people do! But seriously, I realize that it can be tough, but at least you found someone special. So, *congratulations!* A long-distance romance is the next best thing to being there!

You both are in this "apartness" together. And committing to that togetherness—along with a little planning and creativity—means you CAN have a life together while apart.

Since this book is not about relationship counselling, I'd like you now to ask yourself this question: "If it weren't for the distance factor, would this relationship be worthwhile to me?" If you answer yes, I invite you to read on. My commitment to you is that we will enhance the romance in your LDR…beginning today!

So here's to love *in absentia!*

CHAPTER 1

You Are Not Alone

Nobody prefers to be in an LDR over a same-town romance, but LDRs have been going on and succeeding for thousands of years.

It has been estimated that as many as 40 million Americans (one in three workers) have jobs that involve travel. How often? Well over 200 million business trips per year. And about 2.4 million marriages involve one spouse living and working in a different city, according to 1998 U.S. Census Bureau figures.

LDR GLOSSARY: A "California Widow" in 19th Century America was a woman who lost her man to the Gold Rush for a few years.

Just to get a little perspective here (since misery loves company!) you might be interested in learning why *so many* people find themselves in LDRs...

- Rural and small town singles have few available prospects locally
- Business travelers (two-thirds of whom are men) are separated from their lovers on average 3 to 4 days per trip, exposing those travelers who are single to having a lover in another town
- The Internet easily takes the search for a lover beyond your city limits
- Working couples are often separated when one takes a job in another city
- Vacation flings continue as long-distance flames
- Military, political and diplomatic staffers on duty have lovers back home
- College students keep up with their hometown sweethearts and summer loves
- Athletes, journalists and performers spend weeks at a time on the road
- Over a million people are incarcerated, over half of whom are married, separated or supporting others
- People want to date people in a city they're interested in moving to.

Ever since the first hunting and gathering expeditions, people have found themselves separated from their clan. Crusaders locked chastity belts on their wives before going off for months at a time. New England wives paced "widow's walks" on their rooftops, looking out to sea for their husbands' returning ships. And the popular tunes of the first two World Wars brimmed with anticipation for Johnny to come marching home.

There are countless variations of LDRs nowadays...

- Some couples in LDR's start off both living in the same town before one moves away or starts travelling a lot.
- Other couples begin their romance while living in separate towns.
- Some couples might be dating casually. Others are married.
- Some visit one another in person frequently; while others can't afford the expense or take off the time to visit so often.

So long as you're truly in love and you plan to be together eventually, this Guide will help you manage the distance. I've seen too many loves survive the distance to doubt that it can work. And with the Internet spreading, LDR's are growing more prevalent. So many people have lovers at the other end of the rainbow, the globe is virtually covered in criss-crossing colors!

CHAPTER 2

Benefits of an LDR

"Absence makes the heart grow fonder."

Sextus Propertius [54 BC–2 AD]

Let's get in the habit of looking at the bright side, shall we?

Most of my clients realized, often in hindsight after they were reunited with their lovers, that the distance factor had actually brought with it considerable benefits. That's why it's even been proposed over the years that a period of separation be a requirement for a marriage license.

So when doubt and heartache strike, read on to remind yourself of all the good that comes from hearts being apart...

GREATER APPRECIATION FOR EACH OTHER. If you spend a lot of time apart, you'll naturally relish the time once you're back together—especially if it's only for a short time. After a long absence, you'll be less likely to take your time together for granted. You'll appreciate even the little things about your lover much more acutely.

FORCES YOU TO HAVE A LIFE. When you're not sitting around by the phone waiting to hear from your lover, you get up and make things happen for yourself. You're tending to one schedule instead of two. Rather than keeping activities on hold pending your lover's interest and availability, you go out and do things for yourself. This can lead to greater individual success and happiness which can only make you a better catch for your lover.

BROADENS YOUR HORIZONS. Being in an LDR gives you a new definition of community—from Internet friends to people in your lover's town. Relationships often involve two addresses initially, but when they're actually in different cities, you find yourself a semi-resident of a new town. Discovering a new town can lead to new interests and a new awareness. People might bemoan their hectic travel schedule, but in the same breath, they're proud to be bi-coastal.

RETAINS YOUR INDIVIDUALITY. LDRs help people retain their individuality by not fusing them as one the way local relationships might. You have different cities linked to your identities, such that one might be the Southerner and the other the Yankee. And when you get visited, it's fun to show your lover around "your turf." Independence can strengthen character, which in turn can strengthen the relationship.

PROVES YOUR LOVER CARES. If someone's willing to endure the distance to stay in a relationship with you, you've found yourself someone who really cares. No matter how difficult it is for you, there should be great consolation in the fact that someone else is making the same sacrifice for you.

IMPROVES COMMUNICATION. Being apart gives you time to think something through on your own. And when you do speak, the distance seems to facilitate candor. Discussing things from afar can lend an air of detachment that makes you speak your mind more freely. And when you have time restrictions on a daily phone call, you tend to be efficient and to the point. You become better communicators!

HIGHER HIGHS. If you approach the time apart from your lover as extended foreplay, the eventual connection can be pretty dynamic! People call it the "Honeymoon Effect," and it's a way LDRs can keep the passion level higher over time.

GIVES YOU SPACE. LDRs literally give people their space. If you're away for a month on a research project, maybe it's best not to have the daily distraction of a lover. Some people actually maintain separate residences in the same apartment building just to have their own space. Hey, even Ricky and Lucy had separate beds! On a temporary or occasional basis, space can do a duo good.

INCREASES COMMUNICATION. "We TALK so much when my lover is on the road—way more than when we're together," a client told me. Being apart can make you lonely and even insecure; that makes you want to reach out all the more to make contact with your lover. People who spend a lot of time together might take communication for granted and talk less than those who are apart. All of this non-physical contact forces you to become friends, too, not just lovers.

KEEPS THINGS CASUAL (IF YOU WANT.) If you're not yet ready to commit either to a full-time relationship or a shared living arrangement, then an LDR might work just fine for you. Especially if you're both focused on your careers for now, or if you're both interested in seeing other people.

NO PRESSURE FOR SEX (IF YOU WANT.) Some people don't want to have sex before they marry, either for religious, ethical or health reasons. That makes LDRs an ideal arrangement—no possibility for physical contact, and less temptation.

EXTENDS THE RELATIONSHIP. Many say that LDRs allow a relationship to last longer than if the lovers were together. A same-city romance that would last for about 3 months might go on for years if drawn out long-distance. That's probably because living separately or traveling a lot puts less "mileage" on your relationship, pushing back the ultimate end date (if there is to be one.) But hey, if you're using this Guide to live your LDR fully every day, in love and in touch, you can rack up almost as much quality time as if you were living together.

CHAPTER 3

Keys to a Successful LDR

A successful LDR is one in which you grow together while apart, every day until you eventually return or live together.

Research was conducted on family separation during the Persian Gulf War by Fred Medway, a professor of psychology at the University of South Carolina in Columbia. Dr. Medway believes that those who are most likely to fare well (from separation through reunion) are those whose grew up "securely attached"—meaning that they enjoyed a trusting, loving, consistent and available parental influence. Fortunately, he assures me, only about one in four people appears to have difficulty separating from others based on their early attachment history.

There's no single path to success, but I've observed a few common features among most LDRs that worked. The more features you two share from the following list, the more likely your LDR is to succeed.

BEING IN LOVE. Being in love (not just loving the person) is what it seems to take to last and thrive in an LDR. Of those I coached who made it work, none ever doubted the love. But even being in love, that alone is not enough for success long-distance…

EQUAL COMMITMENT. You must both be committed, *explicitly* committed, to keeping the relationship alive during the time apart. You need a passion FOR the relationship (not just IN the relationship.) Both of you must make an equal effort—meeting each other half way virtually cuts the distance in half.

TRUST & FAITH. You must trust your lover since you're rarely there in person to assess things for yourself. Trust will diffuse paranoia and jealousy, two impulses which can be especially destructive from afar. I've actually had clients return to organized religion in order to strengthen their "faith muscle." Being faithful yourself makes it easier to have faith in your lover. (See Chapter 19, "The Monogamy Issue")

HONESTY. Lying has no place in any relationship. But it's probably easier to tell the occasional white lie when you're far away from one another. There's no body language to give you away. No chance of your lover stumbling upon questionable numbers lying around. But I've found that even a small lie in an LDR, when uncovered, is compounded by the distance—you're not there to look your lover in the eye to explain and apologize and promise it won't happen again. All of this means it's especially important to make the "promise to be honest" before you part.

AUTHENTICITY. Distance makes it easy to perpetuate a fantasy. You need to put your real self out there, warts and all, so that when you're together, there are no surprises. Tell your lover about the changes you might be going through. Share your ups as well as your downs. Don't hide your moods or create a rose-colored virtual reality for your lover. Putting it all out on the table nets you familiarity and intimacy.

HEIGHTENED SENSITIVITY. Distance makes for a certain sensory deprivation. If you only talk on the phone for a half-hour each night, you must listen "with your eyes wide open." Imagine what your lover must look like while you're conversing. Be especially attuned during these limited interactions. Articulate your hunches.

CLEAR & FREQUENT COMMUNICATION. Ambiguity and passivity might speak volumes when you're together, but they can be confusing or misleading when you're apart. If it's hard enough pulling something out of your lover in person, you might have to make an extra effort long-distance. Don't sign off and stew over what your lover really meant. It's imperative to let your lover know where you are in your head. Your lover isn't there to observe your body language. Speak up about the same things you want your lover to share with you. If you've had a bad day or don't have long to talk, be up front with your lover as soon as you start that day's conversation. Before hanging up or logging off, try to set a time you'll next try to touch base. The sense of continuity is comforting.

SUPPORT SYSTEM. It's essential that you have friends and relations who'll listen to your joys and frustrations and do things with you since you're "alone but not looking." Many people who really struggle in their LDRs turn to RomanceInstitute.com for ongoing support through romance coaching. Since you're not the only person ever to struggle in an LDR, there's no reason to reinvent the wheel that gets you through it. (See Chapter 6, "Support System")

OCCASIONAL VISITS. You need to physically connect every so often to ground the romance. "Virtual" relationships need to be unplugged as often as possible. At least try to arrange business travel and vacations to bring you together, maybe even half-way between your towns. (See Chapter 16, "Short Visits")

HAVE A LIFE OF YOUR OWN. Have a full, satisfying life when you're apart. Don't just keep busy—really accomplish things that matter to you. Especially consider getting involved in activities or charities which your lover wouldn't care to join in on anyway. If you're a more complete person when solo, it can only improve your romance together.

VIRTUAL SEX. Now's the time to shed the shyness (if there is any) and start talking each other through sexual experiences on a regular basis. Whether it's on the phone, through snail mail or online, "virtual sex" can help maintain intimacy, satisfaction and fidelity…and expand horizons for when you're back together in the flesh.

AMPLE RESOURCES. Airline tickets, phone bills and care packages make an LDR rather costly. It helps if it's not a pinch to be able to overnight a dozen long-stems after you two have had a major meltdown. Without a lover to come home to each night, you'll have the extra time to make some extra cash by putting in some overtime, taking a second job or just focusing on advancing your career.

EXTRA EFFORT. Whatever is said and done locally will probably take a bit more effort to accomplish across the miles. But it's a two-way highway, and knowing that the person you're in love with is doing the same for you should make it all worth it. You're in this for the long haul, regardless of the long distance. Your lover should be meeting you halfway in this department.

HAVE AN END IN SIGHT. It really helps to have a plan for eventually being together. Part of what makes an LDR manageable is knowing that the distance is not going to last forever. Remember, being apart is just the foreplay! Unless we're talking about a spouse in prison, there is no reason to endure a relationship which only offers an endless separation.

CHAPTER 4

Rituals

"I dote on his very absence."

from **The Merchant of Venice** by William Shakespeare

Ritualizing even the simplest activity can make it a surprisingly powerful, satisfying and even transcendent experience.

I've come up with a few simultaneous, directional and nurturing rituals that make lovers present...by their very absence! You don't have to be telepathic to be moved by these small but sweet and often moving gestures.

SIMULTANEOUS RITUALS

TWINKLING EYES. No matter where your lover is, you both share the same big sky. Gaze out a window when you talk on the phone. Look to the sun or moon or across the sea to one another. Make a wish upon the North Star. You can even name a star after one another, or "buy" two stars from your local planetarium that can be "officially" named after you both. Or just give each other glow-in-the-dark stars to stick on the ceiling above your beds! *How I wonder where you are…*

DOUBLE BUBBLE BATH. Take a bath at the same time in your respective tubs. But before you do, make sure that you each have the same scented bath oil or incense. Talk to one another by floating candlelight on the phone while luxuriating in the suds.

MOMENTARY LAPSE OF SOLITUDE. Plan to set aside times or moments of the day to think of one another or do something simultaneously while apart. Maybe whisper one another's name when you each lie down to sleep or when you first awaken—like the Bacharach/David song says, "I say a little prayer for you". And speaking of songs, maybe hum "your song" during sunsets. Or cross your fingers whenever you notice it's noon. When you both know you're doing it, it just about puts you side by side.

BURNING CANDLES AT BOTH ENDS. Have a candle which you light when you want to recall your lover. Light it whenever you communicate with one another on the phone or computer. Or have an appointed time when you're both going to light your respective candles and make love alone. After all, fire is thought to evoke romance more than any other element.

AUDIENCE SHARES. Watch TV or a video at the same time while staying on the phone or Internet together. This lets you share the experience while making ongoing commentary. You can laugh, catcall and swoon together—without having to share your popcorn!

DIRECTIONAL RITUALS

FIND YOUR "C-SPOT". There's a very special place waiting to be discovered—in your home, that is! It's the wall or corner "closest" to your lover's home. That's your "C-spot." Hang a photo or momento there, or maybe a stool to sit upon and reflect. Even when you can't look *into* your lover's eyes, you should always be able to look *toward* them.

SMILES APART. How many miles apart are you and your lover? That's a magic number for you both. Use it in poems, gifts, etc. Copy "I love you" that many times into an e-mail. Embrace the distance by having fun with this number. If you're online, you can compute the distance "as the crow flies" by inputting both of your towns at the website *www.indo.com/distance/index.html.*

BLOW-A-KISS COMPASS. Once you've determined the direction of your lover's city from yours, mark it with a dot of red paint on the face of a compass. You can even get snazzy compasses that wear like watches. Or stick a ball compass on your dashboard or nightstand. That way you'll always know which way to face when blowing kisses!

NURTURING RITUALS

PLANTS. Plants make great gift exchanges between lovers in LDRs. They offer you a daily outlet for your urge to nurture. Watering and caring for the plant becomes a time to reflect on your lover. Options range from a low-maintenance plant (especially if you travel a lot) to a temperamental orchid requiring lots of TLC.

PETS. Like plants, pets involve commitment and require caregiving. But with pets the emotional involvement is obviously greater. And they serve as surrogate children for you and your lover to discuss. Pets offer you an at-home relationship, a reliance, that involves growth and wellness. A popular option among romantics is to keep two lovebirds.

VISIT YOUR LOVER'S FAMILY OR FRIENDS. Spending time with your lover's family or friends (if they're local to you) helps keep your lover present. Developing a real concern and affection for them eventually takes this beyond the function of ritual. These relationships can actually broaden your understanding of and love for your lover.

"When my boyfriend moved for a job, he was concerned about leaving his father behind in a nursing home. I told him I'd visit his dad once a week, and I can't tell you how much that has meant to him. And to his dad! I've actually been going more often lately because his dad and I have totally bonded. He has the same sense of humor as his son!"

Kristy, 46

CHAPTER 5

Dream about Your Lover

" 'Tis distance lends enchantment to the view,
and robes the mountain in its azure hue."

from **Pleasures of Hope** (1799) by Thomas Campbell

Meeting your distant lover in your dreams—that's one sure way to awaken with a smile on your face!

But apart from swapping pillow cases (See Chapter 11, "Care Packages"), how proactive can you be? Wouldn't it be great to call your lover and plan your "Dream Dream" together?

Well, John T. Cox, doctor of Clinical Hypnotherapy in Reston, VA (and an LDR veteran himself) says you can. He cites two approaches for inducing dreams about one another: (1) "The Dream-maker", in which one person talks the other off to sleep while suggesting a dream; and (2) "Dream Planning", in which you both create a dream to have before going to sleep.

To begin the first approach, usually the person who is more stressed out or in need of a good dream is designated the "Dreamer"; the other partner is the "Dream-maker."

(1) SETTING THE MOOD. Leave a light on outside your bedroom, even if you can't see it through the closed door. Get comfortable in bed and call one another. The Dream-maker should be playing music audible to the Dreamer over the phone. When choosing music, long tones (stretched-out notes) encourage a relaxed, dreamy state. Ideally, that's about 50 to 60 beats per minute. (Most music is about 120 beats per minute.) For example, Pachelbel's Canon in D is about the right pace.

(2) ENTERING A DREAMY STATE. The Dream-maker is responsible for talking the Dreamer down from their day into a half-awake, or *hypnogogic*, state. The Dream-maker—speaking slowly, softly and with lots of expression—suggests that the Dreamer visualize stress as a single object which is moving further and further away. Both of you should be breathing deeply and evenly and talking at a similarly slow rate, although the Dreamer shouldn't have much (if anything) to say. Then the Dream-maker, using the *progressive relaxation* technique, suggests that the Dreamer imagine each body part relax, moving from the toes up to the head. String your sentences into one continuous suggestion using the words AND, WHILE and AS...

> *While you are lying there in your bed and hearing the sounds of my voice as you begin to notice the feel of the sheets and the softness of your pillow you can begin to drift along with my words into a beautiful dreamy place..."*

The Dreamer is encouraged to pay attention to physical things (not emotional things) which they normally don't pay attention to, such as how the pillow feels under their head, how the sheets feel across their thighs, how their feet feel different without shoes now...

(3) COMPOSING THE DREAM. The Dream-maker describes the dream scenario in detail, leading the Dreamer into a dream about a place they would like to go, maybe incorporating things they'd like to do. The Dream-maker should consider whether the Dreamer is more visual, auditory or kinesthetic (feeling), and tailor descriptions toward that response. Maybe it's a guided exploration of what you would do with their body, lying in bed together, how you would hold them, slowly describing the details. Maybe it's a shared recollection or a new fantasy. For example, you might guide the Dreamer on a hike up a hill, describing the streams and flowers and birds along the way, to watch a sunset from the top...once there you camp out under the stars...as a warm breeze blows you make love...

(4) HANGING UP THE PHONE. After hearing the dream described in such lulling tones, the Dreamer might be too relaxed to hang up the phone. The Dream-maker should suggest that the Dreamer take a deep breath and reach over and hang up the phone, then drift off into the dream. Neither of you need even say goodnight...

The next morning, even if the Dreamer doesn't remember having the dream, that doesn't mean they didn't dream it! You never know, so don't deprive your dreaming self the pleasure—try it! And regardless of whether or not you recall the dream, it's simply an exquisite way to be lulled to sleep.

It's a good idea to take turns being Dreamer and Dream-maker, so that you experience both sides of this delight. And you can each make an audiotape of yourselves acting as Dream-maker for the other to listen to at will (and not have to worry about hanging up the phone!)

If you both want to compose the dream together (i.e. "Dream Planning"), just guide one another into the hypnogogic state and let the call be more interactive throughout. Propelling one another through a beautiful dream is as exciting as it is peaceful.

You'll find that this experience builds trust, intimacy and some awfully good vibrations. It's a dream come true for lovers apart!

CHAPTER 6

Support System

*"Even when a friend is absent
he is present none the same."*

Marcus Tullius Cicero (106–43 B.C.)

Surrounding yourself with a group of people who want your LDR to succeed is more important than most people realize. After all, you're probably spending more time with them than with your lover.

A support system can consist of family and friends, both men and women. It can also include your therapist, counsellor or personal coach. Even your travel agent has a vested interest in seeing your LDR succeed!

And let's not forget about pets and plants, whether they're yours or your lover's for which you're caring. In supporting them, you in turn ready yourself for receiving support and comfort "from the universe," as they say.

ADVANCE NOTICE. Warn your friends before your lover is about to return that you might be out of touch for a while. Promise to make it up to them with a lunch once your lover is gone.

FRIENDS' AGENDAS. If you and your lover don't live in the same town, people are going to be forever asking you when one of you plans to move to the other's town. It's natural for friends and family to want lovers to be together, just as they might push for marriage. Let them know that you'll let them know when you know—and don't feel bad about making a gracious request that they slow the requests for updates.

NAYSAYERS. Some friends or family members will discourage you from continuing the LDR. Get the naysayers to meet your lover so they can at least respect (and hopefully befriend) one another. Even if it means including them for a meal during a short visit. Seeing you two so happy together should turn them around. Get them to appreciate what goes into a long-distance commitment and why it's worth it—they should grow to respect your extra effort, not dismiss it as futile. I had a clever client send the following pledge to her friends to sign:

"Pledge of the LDR Supporter"

For as long as my friend is in an LDR,
I will offer support, encouraging advice and a
    sounding board.
Never thinking to question their commitment,
Never feeling put off when they blow me off to
    be alone on short visits,
I will downplay the downside of distance, not
    draw attention to it,
Because they'll be so happy if it works out,
And my friend would do the same for me.

Even once you and your lover move in together, you
might find that you're leaving behind family and friends
in your old town. That makes those people your new
long-distance relationships! So, keep in mind some of
the non-amorous principles of distance management in
this Guide—it will help you keep them close, too.

CHAPTER 7

Journals

"I do perceive that the old proverbs be not always true,
for I do find that the absence of my Nath doth breed in me
more continual remembrance of him..."

Lady Ann Bacon [1528–1610] letter to Lady Jane Cornwallis
(regarding the proverb, "Out of sight, out of mind.")

Toss out your Little Black Book with all the names and numbers from your single days—now that you're in love, and in an LDR, it's time to start maintaining a Little "Red" Book!

Your Little Red Book is a journal where you jot down reminiscences, the "must share" moments your lover missed out on by being away.

Sharing the little things that happen in the course of a day make your lover feel truly a part of your life. But being little things, you might forget them in the excitement, and sometimes the rush, of your occasional phone call.

Remember, actual memories from your day (e.g., "I thought of you when I tried to use chopsticks!") pluck at the heartstrings with greater resonance than mere generalizations (e.g., "I thought of you all day.")

You can also use your Little Red Book to jot down ideas for letters, poems or e-mails you might send. Write down new things, new songs that might interest your lover. You might even want to swap Little Red Books with your lover if you're both keeping one.

CHAPTER 8

Love Letters

"Oh heart! oh blood that freezes, blood that burns!"

Robert Browning (1812–1889)

For centuries letters have helped bridge the distance between lovers. Throughout literature, from the medieval epistolary novels to the love poems of the Brownings—we've all swooned at written words coming from lovers' hearts.

The flowery language associated with love letters probably tends to keep most people from even trying to write one. Writing love letters needs to be approached with warmth and confidence, not with a foreboding sense of literary inadequacy. And the letters themselves must speak with truth, clear meaning and modern idiom. In other words, just write like you speak and you'll do fine.

"I never wrote a love letter in my life. Then my girlfriend moved away for school and said I had to write her. Every week, she said, and she even gave me stamped and addressed envelopes. I just crank them out like homework every Sunday morning. They're not poetry or anything, but she says they make her cry. Only thing is I wish she wouldn't save them!"

Mark, 19

PERSONALIZED STATIONERY. Customize the look of the letters you send. Copy a photo (or reduce a collage of photos) of the two of you onto the top of your stationery. Or have an artistic friend render a caricature of you both to top off your letterhead. You can even simply staple sentimental items (like matchbooks or candy wrappers) to the paper from your lover's last visit.

DOUBLE-VALUE COUPONS. Include a handmade "coupon" with your letters, good for a foot massage, breakfast in bed, etc., when you reunite. A coupon is particularly "valuable" when it's something your lover wants from you…possibly something risqué which you are usually reluctant to oblige!

BREAKFAST SERIAL. Send a bunch of individually sealed letters tied together in one package. Explain that your lover can't open each letter until the date on each separate envelope. This "serialized" approach allows you to build anticipation by, say, drawing out a fantasy story over several cards. It gives your lover something to look forward to each day.

FINISHING TOUCHES. Before you seal the envelope, toss in something to make it special: heart-shaped confetti, rose petals, a *bouquet garni* of aromatic herbs. If you're daring, insert a pinch of glitter ("because you put sparkle in my day")—its "staying power" will have your lover thinking of you all day! Trace your hand over the back of the letter you've just written—that way your lover gets to hold your hand after reading it.

ME AND MRS. WALKER. Bill had been Mrs. Walker's milkman for 43 years when Mr. Walker died. At that time it was revealed to the Walker's adult children that their mother and "Bill the Milkman" had been exchanging daily love letters among the milk bottles all those many years. But neither had ever spoken so much as a word of their deep mutual love to the other, let alone acted upon it. The night after Mr. Walker's funeral Bill began sleeping in the house. But before the lovers-to-be went to bed, they lit a fire and burned both of their stacks of love letters in the fireplace—six a week for over four decades—a burning that had long ago been agreed to...in writing.

LOOKING BACK. When you don't feel like writing a letter, take a moment to review past letters you've sent and received. Seeing where you've been and how far you've come can be reassuring and highly satisfying.

CHAPTER 9

Telephone

"But you're from outa town!
The phone bills would just be—!"

Geena Davis trying unsuccessfully to resist seduction
by (alien) Jeff Goldblum in the film **Earth Girls are Easy**

In days of old, talking long-distance on the phone meant white sound, slow articulation and taking care not to talk over one another. So right off the bat, you can be thankful that calls now make lovers sound like they're next door.

You can perceive a lot from a phone call. You can't edit what you say like you might when sending instant messages on-line. And you can get a lot from hearing your lover's vocal inflections and breathing.

Being in an LDR usually means spending a lot of time on the phone, so you might want to determine your usage and research different long-distance phone rates. Like the celebrity hawkers say, the savings do add up—especially if you're prone to cross-country pillow talks deep into the night.

"I would sleep with my cordless phone!"

> *A new bride on the **New York Times** wedding page, re her fiancé who lived half a globe away*

WAKE UP, SLEEPY HEAD! On mornings when you have to wake up extra early, where you might consider using a pay service to awaken you, have your lover call instead. What better way to start the day than to hear the voice you've been dreaming of! (You can even get an alarm clock in which your lover can personalize the wake-up message.)

OUR TIME. Calling at a preset time every day (for the once-a-day callers) makes for something to look forward to, and brings security and comfort. The regularity allows both of you to plan to clear your heads and your desks so you can be fully present. Others in LDRs call much more frequently, from the workplace to the car to home. Or maybe you do most of your catching up on weekends. But no matter when you call, please refrain from multitasking (even if you think you're good at it!) When your lover is far away, it's best to give your full attention and not take anything for granted.

VARY THE CALL LENGTHS. If you have to limit the duration of your calls, you might want to consider doing fewer calls so you can have a long call every so often. Short calls are good for a quick catch-up, but you also need some "quantity time" to really scratch the surface and delve into matters.

TOUCHING BASE VS. TOUCHING HEARTS. If your expectations for a call are playful and romantic, but your lover is just touching base, you're going to hang up unsatisfied. This sort of imbalance is common and usually only a function of differing circumstances. Just tell your lover, before you sign off this time, that you'll need some lovey-dovey talk next time. If you two don't yet say "I love you," just recall a fond remembrance to warm their heart before signing off.

CALLING CARDS. Consider purchasing phone cards to keep your phone bill down. If your lover is strapped for cash, include a few phone cards in your next letter. Even if your lover is rich, you can still write a sexy question on a calling card—insisting that your lover use the card in a public phone booth to address that private query!

PHONE LOVEMAKING. I have a conservative client who would never have considered phone sex with her partner. But they were both growing frustrated with the distance and the lack of sex (they were committed to monogamy). She thought the idea of "phone sex" sounded demeaning, so I suggested that she simply recall some of their most enjoyable sexual experiences with him. Don't think of it as pornographic, just talk about what you enjoy in your lovemaking together. They started off slowly, and things took off from there! Their tele-lovemaking sessions have even improved their ability to be both vocally and physically expressive during their in-person sessions.

DON'T PUSH ANY BUTTONS. Try to avoid the hot topics which you KNOW will always start a fight ("red button" issues, like ex's and politics) or bring you down ("blue button" issues, like loneliness and frustration.) If it's something you simply must discuss, write it in an email or letter or wait until you're face-to-face. Once a button is pushed, the phone call is likely to end flatly and leave a bad taste until your next call.

SILENCE IS GOLD. If you and your distant one go to sleep at the same time, you can do no better than being one another's last call of the day. And as your words fade into yawns, that's your cue to start wrapping things up. You don't want to be awakened hours later to the familiar sound of snoring...coming over the phone from Brazil or some far-off land!

CHAPTER 10

Internet

Let your fingers do the talking! Whether communicating in real-time through "instant messages" or through e-mail, keeping in touch on-line is relatively cheap. Be thankful that most Internet Service Providers (ISPs) now provide unlimited usage for a monthly fee.

Here are a few ways to keep your lover in your web <g>...

E-MAILS. This is the cheapest, fastest way to convey the most info. Remember to save the e-mails you send one another—bind them and send them to your lover as a gift. And remember, less can be more, so try sending an e-mail with just one set of double quotes (") on it to symbolize your togetherness. Develop your own affectionate style of being "graphic."

"Sometimes we'll type with our tongues or noses. We'll even kiss the mouse to click it to send the message. It looks like silly gibberish, but it's like our own love language!"

Stella, 28

LOVERS WEBPAGE. Some long-distance lovers create their own webpage. Sort of like carving your initials on a tree together. You can leave each other e-mails, post pictures and, basically, be seen in public together! You can even install a countdown clock to display the days, hours and minutes until you both connect in person with freeware from *nestersoft.hypermart.net/timeleft/*

ONLINE CARDS. Some ISPs make sending a sweet note easy (and automatically regular) by offering e-mail greeting cards. If it's someone you just met and want to woo anonymously, try *SecretAdmirer.com*.

SWEET NOTHINGS. Attach voice documents to your e-mail's. Or add chat sounds (called WAV's.) That way your lover can listen to your "sweet nothings" when online. Also, check out *ICQ.com*.

SLUMBER PARTY. Plan to stay up all night on-line, communicating with your lover via instant messages. Buy the same food or drink in advance, so you're both feasting on the same munchies.

I-GAMES. Some ISP's offer interactive games, such as checkers or backgammon, to be played online. So you can spend a Saturday night playing parlor games with your cross-country lover.

VIDEOCONFERENCING. With a camera attachment, you can see one another while cybering. Or go rent a videoconference room for a *tête-à-tête*. Look in the phone book under meeting centers, conferencing centers or teleconferencing.

Remember, relating only via cyber is fantasy. If you've met someone on-line, I'd strongly advise you to meet in person (in a public place) before developing any emotional attachment. Don't prolong the fantasy via computer or phone. Avoid surprises by meeting one another face-to-face early on so you can begin the relationship in earnest.

CHAPTER 11

Care Packages

"Presents endear absents."

Charles Lambe [1775–1834]

Ah, those brown paper packages tied up with strings! Nothing warms the cockles of a lonely heart like an unexpected special delivery from your lover...even if you had to facilitate it by supplying your lover with a stack of labels with your name and address.

This is the aspect of LDRs where we separate the givers from the takers. Heck, even the astronauts on the Mir space station were rocketed care packages every two to three months. It's an essential element of distance management: touching through stuff.

It might help to befriend a friend or neighbor of your lover's. Someone to secretly do the occassional footwork of, say, tucking a card under your lover's windshield wiper. When a surprise package comes via means other than the mailbox, it scores big romance points!

Of course, if your lover mentions in passing that they need something simple like a new toothbrush or umbrella, that's your shopping list. But it's always sweet to embellish the package with a little something extra...

A PART OF ME. There are many momentos which you can prepare for your lover that will conjure up your physical presence...

- Cast a body part (face, hand, etc.) and send it. Home kits are available from some hobby shops. If it is something that might be handled frequently, cast it in rubber or something less fragile than plaster. This way you can hold hands (or anything else) as often as you like!
- Have a professional photographer take your picture, or commission some budding artist to paint your portrait.
- Have a hologram of your face made. (Inquire at your local science museum for the names of local hologram artists.)

- Swap locks of hair tied in a bow or leather string. Affix them to a photograph.
- Send him a lipstick imprint on a photo. Frame it so it won't smear, or laminate it and attach a magnet to the back so it can go on the fridge.

TIME SHARE SWAPS. Sleep on a pillow case for a couple of nights and send it to your lover. Have your lover do the same for you. You can even get a photo of your face imprinted onto the pillow case. That way you'll see and smell one another as you drift off to sleep. Try temporarily swapping other items as well, such as blankets and hairbrushes.

"My boyfriend left his favorite faded denim shirt once. It smells like him. Sometimes I sleep with it. I even took it with me on a business trip. I guess you never outgrow the need for a security blanket!"

Marla, 32

PUZZLING PIECES. Get a photo reproduced onto puzzle pieces. Many local photo developers offer this service. Mail a few pieces of the puzzle to your lover each day to let the anticipation build. Once-a-day "serialized deliveries" give your lover something to look forward to. The photo might be of you holding a special message to your lover, or you could write the message on the back.

LOVE SHRINE KIT. Send your lover a kit to build a romantic shrine to you on a tabletop or in a desk drawer. Include a photo of yourself, a lock of hair, your favorite book of poems. Maybe even a voodoo doll with your perfume/cologne on it! Your lover can add items to the shrine over time. It can be romantic, humorous, erotic—whatever you want.

ROMANTIC DINNER FOR ONE. Ship an overnight package to your lover that includes everything necessary for a candlelit meal. That means a homemade, frozen meal (with microwave instructions); candles; a photo; a flower or corsage; a handmade music tape; and maybe homemade fortune cookies—with personalized fortunes. Include a few sealed notes for your lover to open at different stages in the meal…and one for afterwards.

BALLOONS IN A BOX. Ship your lover 2 mylar balloons in a box. They retain their helium longer than rubber balloons. It couldn't be cheaper (or more lightweight!) to ship. And when opened, someone's in for an in-their-face surprise!

LOTSA CATALOGUES. If you're not already a catalogue junkie, it's time to become one now that you're in an LDR! From gifts to food, catalogs are the shopping mall for LDRs. Also, gourmet stores and specialty vendors will often ship for you—that takes care of any special shipping needs (like dry ice) and any border restrictions.

Product "of-the-month" clubs (from beer to nuts) are a good way to keep the love a-comin' on a regular basis.

SLICE O' BURNING LOVE. If your lover happens to mention being hungry while you two are on the phone, log onto the Internet. Many pizza companies list locales on their web sites. Before you even hang up, your Hungry One will be answering the door for a surprise delivery. Use the final section of the Guide ("Your Lover's Profile") to list your lover's delivery services.

SCRAP BOOK. After you visit one another, save keepsakes from your time together. Matches from a romantic restaurant, movie ticket stubs, photographs from the trip, etc. Assemble them all into a scrap book commemorating the trip, and send it to your lover.

SCRAP CALENDAR. Customize a calendar for your lover with quotes (your own or others'), drawings, photos and keepsakes attached to each day. Tell your calendar guy or gal not to peek ahead so that every day can be a surprise!

DAILY AUDIO LOVE DIARIES. Carry around a micro-cassette player and tape yourself, or your surrounding sounds, throughout the day with things your lover would appreciate. Send your lover the tape. This is an especially satisfying gesture when both of you are doing it and exchange tapes (or disks) when you're apart, halfway between your visits.

CANDYGRAM. Buy different kinds of candy with fun brand names. Send your lover the candy along with a note that incorporates the names (e.g., "I am CERTain we are MINT to be together, even if a ROCKY ROAD is ahead.") It shouldn't cost more than $10 to sweeten your honey's day with this customized candygram.

VIDEO STARS. If you each have a video camera, you can send romantic/erotic tapes to one another. But a word to the wise: agree to use the same tape and record over it each time. That way there'll be less to end up on the Internet! Videotape can outlast most relationships, so keep the "tape trail" to a minimum.

Companies are cracking down on personal shipping, so you might not have your workplace mailroom at your disposal. Find out where your nearest overnight shipping office is, along with its deadlines (international can be different from domestic).

Remember always to check that your package was received. Don't assume it was, especially if it was more than a trifle, such as a conciliatory gift after a dispute.

CHAPTER 12

Musical Reminders

"When I need you
I just close my eyes and I'm with you"

from "When I Need You"
by Carole Bayer Sager & Albert Hammond

Making tapes of music for one another is a great way to stay connected. It keeps your lover thinking of you, while you get to set the mood. Of course, if love songs tend to depress you with feelings of longing, program your radio to play only classical, dance or talk stations.

Here are some ideas on how to keep the fires burning through music...

SING ME A LETTER. Send a love letter which incorporates titles of songs in the text. Along with the letter include a compilation tape of the actual songs. Personalize a cover sleeve for the tape or CD.

CHAIR DANCE. While talking on the phone, play a favorite song just loud enough for your lover to hear. Both of you can share a little dance together, spinning around in your respective chairs at work (if you're not seated out in the open!)

THIS GOES OUT TO... Go to *www.discjockey.com* and dedicate love songs to one another while online. Next best thing to the Wurlitzer!

Here are a few songs with at least refrains that pertain to LDRs. You might want to include some of them in a compilation for your lover:

> *"When I Need You" (Leo Sayer)*
> *"Somewhere Out There" (Fievel: An American Tale)*
> *"Get Here If You Can" (Brenda Russell)*
> *"Tie a Yellow Ribbon Round the Ole Oak Tree"*
>   *(Tony Orlando & Dawn)*
> *"Ain't No Mountain High Enough"*
>   *(Marvin Gaye & Tammy Terrell)*
> *"Leaving on a Jet Plane" (Peter, Paul & Mary)*
> *"This is Dedicated to the One I Love"*
>   *(Mommas & the Poppas)*
> *"Open Arms" (Journey)*
> *"Come Back to Me" (Frank Sinatra)*

"Lift the Wings" (RiverDance: The Show)
"Right Here Waiting for You" (Richard Marx)
"When You're Gone (The Cranberries)
"Nothing Else Matters" (Metallica)
"Reunited" (Peaches & Herb)
"Long Distance Love Affair" (Sheena Easton)
"Together Again" (Buck Owens)
"Don't You Love Her When She's Walking Out
*   the Door" (The Doors)*
"Missing You" (John Waite)
"Dream Lover" (Bobby Darin)
"I Want to Hold Your Hand" (The Beatles)
"Don't Want to Miss a Thing" (Aerosmith)
"Someday We'll Be Together"
*   (Diana Ross & the Supremes)*
"In the Wee Small Hours of the Morning"
*   (Carly Simon)*
"When Johnny Comes Marching Home Again"
WWII songs of separation and reunion

If you can think of any songs to add to this list for the next edition, please let us know via our website, *RomanceInstitute.com*. All of our friends in LDRs will benefit from your additions, so we all thank you!

CHAPTER 13

Social Diversions

"If you are idle, be not solitary…"

Samuel Johnson [1779]

What good is sitting alone by the phone? Get out and enrich your life! You don't always need your "other half" to accompany you to public functions or activities. Social abstenance is not a virtue—so come to the cabaret… or wherever!

When you go out and get a life, you gain independence—not from your lover, but from your pining! And that actually benefits LDRs.

So remember, good things come to those who wait… *constructively.* Here are some suggestions on passing the time and making it count…

FRIENDS APLENTY. Increase your base of close friends to socialize with. And weed out the naysayers who think you're wasting your time in an LDR. If your lover has friends near where you live, consider spending time with them, too. That helps keep your love alive among people who respect and encourage the relationship.

LOCAL TOURIST. Play tourist in your own town. If your town is big enough to have a tour book, there are probably activities (e.g., libraries, gardens, museums, churches, tours) which you've never explored. Go with a friend, but don't be afraid to explore them solo—sometimes you get the most out of something when it's at your own pace. That way, next time your lover is in town, especially if it's for a short spell, you'll know exactly where you two should go for a good time (outside of the bedroom, that is!)

PLATONICALLY YOURS. Having platonic friends of the opposite/desired sex can offer you companionship for work functions or benefit events. And if they are also friends with your lover, you might even feel at liberty to hang out with them or go dancing on occasion. There's no reason to miss out on the social fun that couples enjoy.

SING YOUR HEART OUT. Singing is a wonderful form of release from heartache. Since you should always be on the lookout for local activities, consider joining a church choir or local chorus—or if your pipes sound rusty, just let it go in the shower! It might help you plumb the depths and really untie those knots in your stomach.

SCHOOL'S COOL. You've probably got a night or two free each week, so why not take a class? Self-defense, a foreign language, arts and crafts—surely there's something you've always wondered about. Look into it. Like I always coach my clients, improving yourself should only improve the relationship if it's a solid one.

"When I learned that my wife was going to be away for three months on business, I signed up for a course at the community college. I'd been wanting to study landscape architecture for years, and this seemed like the perfect time to focus on it. And she loved what I did with the backyard when she got back home!"

Tom, 27

CHAPTER 14

Physical Diversions

"…if you are solitary, be not idle."

Samuel Johnson [1779]

Physical frustration doesn't just occur from a lack of sex (which is 90% mental anyway), but from a lack of physical affection and nearness, too. This might seem like the gravest downside to an LDR, but there's actually a lot you can do about it. Just devote yourself to diving into these diverse diversions!

STAY HEALTHY FOR YOUR LOVER. If you only get together on occasion, you don't want to spend it in bed…*with the flu!* You two are going to have enough to do and deal with during your visit; physical well-being should be a given. So while you're apart, swap healthy recipes and tips with one another. Never mother one another—that's a *romance no-no!*—but stay involved with one another's health.

WORK IT OUT. Rather than tossing and turning all night in bed alone, spend more waking moments exercising. You'll sleep more soundly. Yoga and swimming seem to be great stress-fighters for those suffering from heartache. Women might even want to look into a self-defense class if you often go around town unescorted (or live alone at home). The residual benefit, of course, is that you'll look better for when you two next reunite!

OH-M-M-M. If exercise isn't for you, consider focusing on the more sensuous or meditative activities. Look into getting regular massages—there are many different styles out there for you to experience. Also try saunas, steam rooms, bubble baths, hot tubs and deep breathing. These activities can help keep you loose, allow you to meditate and help cleanse your spirit. Make the activity regular to really take the edge off.

DANCE CLASS. If you each take the same dance class in your respective towns, when you reunite you can go dancing together and look like you dance together every weekend. Swing, big band, salsa—it's all new again!

FULL CONTACT. If you really miss how your lover takes your breath away, throw yourself into activities which literally knock the wind out of you! Contact sports and team competition can be exhilarating diversions that allow you to actually physically connect with others in a way that provides a wonderful release. See what adult sports leagues (e.g., softball, basketball) exist in your town. You could even get extreme…with boxing!

O SOLE MIO. Masturbation will keep the engine humming. Be creative in how you recall your lover's presence. Or make it an exotic project and take a course in tantric sex.

"Sometimes I lie in my bed and make love to myself…when you are truly in love with someone, you can feel them with you!! We've had a few experiences that were not planned and when we talked about them later, we found out that we had made love by ourselves with each other in mind at the very same time! This is something that I had never considered doing in the past…I sure was missing out!"

Magdalena, 43

Physical diversions can help alleviate your heavy heart. But if you suffer from those melancholy pangs for too long, there could be mental or physical repercussions such as anxiety, depression and weight shifts. You might wish to seek out counseling if you can't shake the heartache.

CHAPTER 15

Arrivals

"Tie a yellow ribbon round the ole oak tree"
Tony Orlando & Dawn [1976]

The return of a long-awaited lover offers romantics their greatest thrill. Just ask the cashier at the airport coffee shop.

NASA psychologists have determined that astronauts should go no longer than six weeks without seeing their lovers. But it's probably safe to say that the longer the separation, the sweeter the arrival.

The triumphant return is my favorite part of a romance novel...*An eighteenth-century woman is atop her home, pacing the widow's walk. She swoons and steadies herself as she spots her husband's ship returning home after many months at sea...* Well, Prudence, heat up the figgy pudding!

The reunion might make one of you feel like a stranger or feel especially needy. Here are a few suggestions to help reorient and steady you both during that adjustment period, as well as to enhance the experience.

ANTICIPATION EMANCIPATION. Keep yourself active the day or two before you see each other. Actually schedule things to fill up your days, especially physical and social activities. Don't be alone or your mind will wander, and the anticipation might build to a point where you develop unrealistic expectations for the upcoming visit.

DON'T ARRIVE EMPTY-HANDED. Have a little something to give your lover when you reunite. A sweet treat, a photo, even if it's a silly little drawing you scribbled on the plane. Maybe plan ahead and send your lover 11 roses in advance of your arrival...bringing the twelfth rose with you to present in-person. Even the smallest gestures can resonate in the heart.

WELL, HELLO! When welcoming back your lover, it's always worth the extra effort to look your best...even if you normally don't fuss with your appearance. So tweak those rosy cheeks! You want your lover's heart to leap at the first sight of you—that's a memory they'll cherish.

SMOOTH REENTRY. If you're the one being visited, prepare as much as possible in advance. Clean your place. Stock the refrigerator. Have gas in the car. Have a paper with listings in case you want to go to the movies, a show or museum. You shouldn't be doing errands during the first few hours that your lover has returned. This is peak romance time!

CHAPTER 16

Short Visits

"It was a delightful visit—perfect, in being much too short."

from **Emma** [1815] by Jane Austen

When you only have a short time together, you naturally want to make the most of it. You want to have a fulfilling visit and do special things. But don't waste time worrying about the imminent departure. You've earned this visit, so enjoy it!

But a word of caution: don't always treat it like a vacation or honeymoon. Don't have your visit be unrealistically fabulous the whole time. You need to leave some time for regular, day-to-day activities. You might have to readjust to one another's routines. You want to keep expectations at a healthy level to prevent let-downs.

Having said that, there ARE some wonderful things to do during a short visit…

THEME WEEKENDS. Add a flavor to your weekends by incorporating a theme from a movie, famous event or celebrity. If shopping and bubble baths are in order, make it a "Pretty Woman" weekend. Or try celebrating Christmas in July. Or maybe salute Frank Sinatra by playing his music and eating at Italian restaurants.

MEMORY GARDEN. If your visits to one another are infrequent, make them special by planting a flower, bush or tree each time before departing. Each plant becomes a living diary of your time together. Love grows!

EVERYDAY MEMORIES. When you two are next together, take photos of one another going through your daily routines. Get shots of your lover doing things like brushing their teeth, frying an egg, sleeping—and display the pictures in your bathroom, kitchen and bedroom, respectively. You can even get a shot of your lover pumping gas to store in your glove compartment!

CONSOLIDATED SOLIDARITY. Have all of your friends/family come over for drinks or a meal, even though you might want your lover all to yourself. If your friends/family are part of your life, and you're always talking about them, your lover might want to occasionally experience them firsthand. If you lived in the same town, it would happen naturally over time, but in a two-town LDR you need to plan it out. They are part of your reality, and visits shouldn't only be hedonistic fantasy with your lover. And it might also be helpful for your friends/family—who try to be supportive of your LDR— to spend some time with your lover.

TAKE A BREATHER. Don't spend every waking moment together, even if the visit is a short one. You need a few minutes apart to catch your breath, get some perspective.

FINAL STRETCH. The final days or hours may be tense with anticipation. Butterflies can lead to tummy aches and irritability. Small things might seem worth fighting over because you're on edge, taking the imminent departure out on one another. You might even think your lover wouldn't leave you if they truly loved you. This is when you need to take a deep breath and savor your remaining time together. It's precious!

SURPRISE VISITS. Is anything more romantic (or possibly more of a fiasco!) than a surprise visit? This leap of faith is only advisable when you really know your lover's schedule. Maybe you know a friend of your lover's with whom to clear things. You might tell your lover to be home at a certain time to receive a special delivery (i.e., you.) That way you'll be sure to see each other—at least initially. Realize that your lover might have weekend plans that can't be changed to include you. Let's just hope you're not surprising one another with surprise visits at the same time!

CHAPTER 17

Departures

"The joy of life is variety; the tenderest love requires
to be renewed by intervals of absence."

from **The Idler** (1758-1760) by Samuel Johnson

Parting can be such sweet sorrow! You want it to be a wonderful departure whose memory will linger for a long while—but without the sudden empty feeling afterwards.

Since sometimes people leave mentally before they leave physically, here are some suggestions to give your send-off a buildup without the letdown.

LAST MEAL. Food is sustenance. Think of sustaining your lover through the upcoming time apart by somehow ritualizing your last meal together. Make it special by memorizing a toast ahead of time. Then maybe you could even feed one another during the meal—it can be as silly as it is romantic. If you have a special "parting gift" (sounds like a game show contestant!), this would be a lovely time to present it.

GOOD-BYE ALREADY! Don't make any plans for your last few hours together before departing. Just hang out. Not that you'd ever get your fill of one another, but idling in each other's company for a while might make the parting easier.

KEEP IT LIGHT. You should have covered all the big issues before departure time—don't put off the big talk until the end! The eleventh hour is the time for leaving a wonderful taste in one another's mouths. You might be on edge before the departure and tend to squabble over trivial matters. So make an extra effort to keep this time respectful and upbeat.

SURPRISE MOMENTO. Always have something special to slip into your lover's suitcase or pocket, or leave around their home, before you part. Your lover might not even find it for a few days after you've parted. Whether it's a box of mints in a medicine cabinet or an elaborate treasure hunt through their house, keepsakes really warm the heart at this fragile juncture in your LDR. This gesture really helps prolong your physical presence, especially when your lover comes to expect it, never knowing when they'll find something in their sock drawer or freezer.

SENSORY LOADING. How do you make a good-bye linger beyond the departure? Load it with the five senses. Lick his lips, smudge his shirt with your perfume, hum a tune, pinch his butt and flash him something visual to remember you by!

LOCATION, LOCATION, LOCATION. Where you part should matter to a true romantic. So whenever possible, I discourage clients from drawn-out goodbyes at airports and train stations. They're too cold and public, which will only make you feel worse once you're left standing there. Say goodbye at home, at a coffeehouse or in a park. Let your lover take a cab. Or maybe a friend of your lover's (whom you wouldn't let elbow in on the visit!) could drive your lover and they can catch up that way. Shaving thirty minutes off of your time together won't diminish your love. You'll be playing that final image of your lover over and over in your mind for the days, weeks or months to come. Let it be special.

WELCOME BACK THERE. Have something awaiting your lover at their home for when they arrive back there. Whether it's something like an email, or a package you slipped into the snail e-mail during your visit together— take care to cushion your lover's re-entry into their home away from your home.

ADVANCE TICKETING. It makes the goodbye easier when you have a date in mind for the next visit. Consider buying blocks of tickets in advance if you can predict when you'll be visiting one another on a regular basis. Get to know a travel agent who can keep you in the loop for airline specials. Or track down web information about online ticket specials yourself.

HIT THE GROUND RUNNING. Plan a wonderful little activity for yourself the moment you are once again alone. Do something social, whether you know the people or not, to take you away from your sudden solo-ness. If you still have any energy left, try something physical (like hitting a driving range, or hiking along a public path.) If you get with a friend, make it one whom you haven't seen in a while, so you can catch up on the last few months—not just on the last few days with your lover! If you were to get with a closer friend at this point, you'd probably just spend the whole time debriefing them on your lover's visit! It's time to get busy again—having a life.

CHAPTER 18

Handling Disputes

Your arm's too short to fight long-distance!

Being away from one another can put you on edge (despite all I've suggested in here!) And that fragile state can set you up to combust more easily than if you were to live closer.

Consider the in-person argument: no matter how it ends, you might want some distance from one another to cool your heels. Well, an LDR certainly gives you space. In fact, your communication together should be so efficient from being in an LDR that you're more likely to resolve things quickly...at least to keep the phone bill down!

But when things do turn edgy, here are some suggestions.

DON'T HANG UP ANGRY. Just as in-person lovers often won't go to bed while still upset with one another, it's ideal for LDR lovers to resolve disputes before hanging up or logging off. But that's not always possible due to the time and financial restraints of being in different places. Keep in mind that the ramifications of a hang-up are much more alienating from afar than if you were to hang up while in the same town. So before you ever argue, agree never to hang up angry. If things are unresolved when it's time to hang up, set a later time to work through it.

ROMANCING THE PHONE. So you're amidst a dispute... Take a deep breath. Slow the pace down. Maybe turn on soothing music. Cradle, don't grip, the phone in your hand. Allow for periods of silence while communicating, maybe even change the topic for a while, then return when tempers have cooled and attempt a resolution.

FOLLOW-UP E-MAIL. After a heated phone call to your lover, sending a follow-up e-mail gives you a chance to compose your thoughts. This way you get more time than the phone might allow. Sometimes it helps to be redundant with follow-up clarifications, compliments and apologies, especially when you only talk on the phone occasionally. You might even tell your lover before hanging up to expect an e-mail so that you both won't stew until the next phone call. In this respect, a dispute can actually be resolved more efficiently long-distance than face-to-face.

NO VIRTUAL BREAK-UPS. Before you get to the melt-down point, make a promise with your lover that you'll never break up from afar. You must come together face-to-face and discuss the matter first. It's harder to throw it all away when you're dealing with the big picture in person. This suggestion has saved several of my clients' romances that went on to become same-city marriages.

LOVE REINFORCEMENT. After a dispute have your lover's favorite catalogue handy to rush a gift off…even if the incident wasn't your fault. A gift creates a tender moment to help heal the pain. Don't think of it as an admission of guilt—it's just a needed reminder of your feelings, a hug by proxy.

CHAPTER 19

The Monogamy Issue

This is where you need to set ground rules once you two are serious. You might already realize this if you've been in a past LDR that didn't work out because of the monogamy issue. As I always coach my clients, the time apart should be regarded as foreplay to when you get back together.

Discuss things openly, but never try to force your lover to adopt your position. Remember the woman whose warrior husband shackled her in a heavy, iron chastity belt before he went off to pillage some far-off land—she ended up running away with the village locksmith! Absence can either make the heart grow fonder, or it can make it go yonder—it depends on how well you manage the distance and use this guide.

When it comes to monogamy, there are both assumptions and commitments. Let's be clear about the distinctions between the two when considering the following options...

(A) **Assume an open relationship.** This is probably how most newer relationships operate before monogamy is comfortably broached. Here you play around with seeming impugnity. Assuming this "don't ask, don't tell" behavior usually works until one of you catches wind of a third party influence. Then at least one of you will probably realize that you would have preferred discussing the issue sooner.

(B) **Assume monogamy.** This works fine so long as you're both on the same wavelength. But who can be sure without a discussion? All too often, after confronting their lover, people hear back, "What did you expect me to do with you two-thousand miles away?" The answer is that you can't expect much so long as you are only operating from assumptions.

(C) **Commit to monogamy.** If you pledge fidelity to one another, you'll have more peace of mind than if you hadn't discussed it. Even if it's stressful to bring up the topic in the first place. This way, if someone is unfaithful, it will be flagged as an outright breach of trust...not just a misunderstanding about one another's positions on the matter.

(D) **Commit to a "don't ask, don't tell" approach.** This allows you to do what you need to do if monogamy is too unbearable during too long a time apart. This works when you both acknowlege you need in-person sex to sustain you, but neither of you wants to hear the other's details. Some of my clients using this approach promise never to get with the same person more than once. Just don't suddenly "ask" or "tell" the details of your private doings during an argument—that's cruel and breaks the commitment.

(E) **Have an open relationship.** Swing like a monkey and make your separate experiences part of your shared sex life by relating them to one another. This is a two-way street, so you better enjoy hearing about your lover's other experiences—even from third parties—not just having your own freewheeling times.

Remember, no matter what your lover does, you can't call it "cheating" unless you've explicitly committed to monogamy.

CHAPTER 20

"Romanspirations"

On each of the following pages through the end of the book, you'll find a reflection designed to boost the romance in your LDR. These "Romanspirations" should inspire you when feelings of heartache and longing creep up.

Jot down what each one means to you on the lines provided. You can write down special memories you shared, quotes from songs, poems, silly notions or lengthy musings. Just don't feel obliged to fill them all out in one sitting; it's best to add to each one over time.

Whether you're adding to them or reading them over, the Romanspirations are designed to give you a pick-me-up. You might even lift some of your Romanspiration writings to record in your journal or "Little Red Book." And since their intention is inspirational, they might even jog your romantic spirit to come up with an original poem or gift idea.

Of course, it would be a wonderful gift to present this Guide to your lover with each of the Romanspirations already partially filled-in by you. That way they can fill in the rest on their own, gaining inspiration from what you already wrote.

SAMPLE OF A "ROMANSPIRATION" PAGE. Let's take the first Romanspiration that follows—"Keeping the home fires burning"—as an example for how someone might fill it in over time.

*"In our LDR, 'keeping the home fires burning' means…*My lover brings me warmth and comfort, so I must return the favor…I should use my fireplace more often. It makes me feel romantic and cozy…I'll fix up my place to be more comfortable for my lover during the next visit…It was a big responsibility for a cave dweller to keep the embers from going out while the clan was out hunting—even though it was probably the hunters who got all the glory!…My house is not a home unless I burn a candle for my lover before I go to sleep…Our love is on fire!…"

Keeping the Home Fires Burning

In our LDR, *keeping the home fires burning* means…

_____

_____

_____

_____

_____

_____

_____

_____

ROMANSPIRATION #2

Truth and Trust Foremost

In our LDR, *truth and trust foremost* means…

_____

_____

_____

_____

_____

_____

_____

_____

ROMANSPIRATION #3

Telepathing Love

In our LDR, *telepathing love* means…

_____

_____

_____

_____

_____

_____

_____

_____

Telepathing Love

_____

_____

_____

_____

_____

_____

_____

_____

_____

_____

_____

_____

_____

_____

_____

_____

_____

_____

_____

_____

ROMANSPIRATION #4

Destiny is Not Geographical

In our LDR, *destiny is not geographical* means…

_____

_____

_____

_____

_____

_____

_____

_____

ROMANSPIRATION #5

Time Apart is Foreplay

In our LDR, *time apart is foreplay* means…

_____

_____

_____

_____

_____

_____

_____

_____

Time Apart is Foreplay

Expanding Horizons

In our LDR, *expanding horizons* means…

_____

_____

_____

_____

_____

_____

_____

_____

Expanding Horizons

_____

_____

_____

_____

_____

_____

_____

_____

_____

_____

_____

_____

_____

_____

_____

_____

_____

_____

ROMANSPIRATION #7

Hearts Grow Fonder

In our LDR, *hearts grow fonder* means…

_____

_____

_____

_____

_____

_____

_____

_____

ROMANSPIRATION #8

Frustration is Fruitless

In our LDR, *frustration is fruitless* means…

_____

_____

_____

_____

_____

_____

_____

_____

Saying a Little Prayer for My Lover

In our LDR, *saying a little prayer for my lover* means…

_____

_____

_____

_____

_____

_____

_____

_____

Saying a Little Prayer for My Lover

Where We Are is a State of Mind

In our LDR, *where we are is a state of mind* means…

_____

_____

_____

_____

_____

_____

_____

_____

Where We Are is a State of Mind

Bettering Ourselves While Apart

In our LDR, *bettering ourselves while apart* means…

_____

_____

_____

_____

_____

_____

_____

_____

ROMANSPIRATION #12

Keeping Hearts Connected

In our LDR, *keeping hearts connected* means...

_____

_____

_____

_____

_____

_____

_____

_____

Longing for Love Only Shortens It

In our LDR, *longing for love only shortens it* means...

_____

_____

_____

_____

_____

_____

_____

_____

Longing for Love Only Shortens It

_____

_____

_____

_____

_____

_____

_____

_____

_____

_____

_____

_____

_____

_____

_____

_____

_____

_____

_____

_____

Distance is Temporary

In our LDR, *distance is temporary* means...

_____

_____

_____

_____

_____

_____

_____

_____

Distance is Temporary

Love Knows No Boundaries

In our LDR, *love knows no boundaries* means…

_____

_____

_____

_____

_____

_____

_____

_____

Removing One Another's Heartache

In our LDR, *removing one another's heartache* means…

_____

_____

_____

_____

_____

_____

_____

_____

_____

_____

_____

_____

_____

_____

_____

_____

_____

_____

_____

_____

_____

_____

_____

_____

_____

ROMANSPIRATION #17

Knowing Love is Out There

In our LDR, *knowing love is out there* means...

_____

_____

_____

_____

_____

_____

_____

_____

_____

_____

_____

_____

_____

_____

_____

_____

_____

_____

_____

_____

_____

_____

_____

_____

_____

_____

_____

Distance Lets Us Connect as Friends

In our LDR, *distance lets us connect as friends* means...

_____

_____

_____

_____

_____

_____

_____

_____

Distance Lets Us Connect as Friends

_____

_____

_____

_____

_____

_____

_____

_____

_____

_____

_____

_____

_____

_____

_____

_____

_____

_____

_____

So Close No Matter How Far

In our LDR, *so close no matter how far* means...

_____

_____

_____

_____

_____

_____

_____

_____

Touching Base

In our LDR, *touching base* means…

_____

_____

_____

_____

_____

_____

_____

_____

Touching Base

_____

_____

_____

_____

_____

_____

_____

_____

_____

_____

_____

_____

_____

_____

_____

_____

_____

_____

_____

_____

Having Encouraging Friends

In our LDR, *having encouraging friends* means…

_____

_____

_____

_____

_____

_____

_____

_____

Having Encouraging Friends

_____

_____

_____

_____

_____

_____

_____

_____

_____

_____

_____

_____

_____

_____

_____

_____

_____

_____

ROMANSPIRATION #22

Keeping The Faith

In our LDR, *keeping the faith* means…

_____

_____

_____

_____

_____

_____

_____

_____

Love Transcends Distance

In our LDR, *love transcends distance* means...

_____

_____

_____

_____

_____

_____

_____

_____

_____

_____

_____

_____

_____

_____

_____

_____

_____

_____

_____

_____

_____

_____

_____

_____

_____

_____

_____

_____

_____

Together Wherever

In our LDR, *together wherever* means…

_____

_____

_____

_____

_____

_____

_____

Love Conquers All

In our LDR, *love conquers all* means...

_____

_____

_____

_____

_____

_____

_____

_____

YOUR LOVER'S PROFILE

Fill out the following information about your lover. Either ask them or find out on your own next time you visit them, or if you're giving this copy of the Guide to your lover, fill it out with your own information and phone numbers. It will help you be there for one another.

Food delivery services: _____

_____

Liquor delivery: _____

Flower delivery: _____

Cake delivery: _____

Chocolate & candy delivery: _____

Masseur/Masseuse: _____

Favorite Radio Station's Dedication Line: _____

Usual Wake-up time: Weekday _____ Weekend _____

Usual Bed time: Weekday _____ Weekend _____

EMERGENCY CONTACT INFORMATION...

Ambulance or EMS: _____

Nearest Hospital: _____

Doctor: _____

Prior Health Conditions: _____

Blood Type: _____

Local Police Department: _____

Local Fire Department: _____

A Close Friend to Contact: _____

A Neighbor to Contact: _____

ABOUT THE AUTHOR

Leslie Karsner, a columnist, speaker and founder of the popular website *RomanceInstitute.com*, says she's been coaching people about romance all of her life—even before she was named "Class Romancer" in high school!

It actually became a career a few years ago when, as an Executive Coach, her clients increasingly focused on romance issues. "I began serving as a professional cheerleader, confidante, and strategist for my clients. But the principles I developed for their romances led them to experience a romance with *all* aspects of their lives," she explains.

Her hundreds of clients have included everyone from Fortune 500 executives to housewives. *Cosmopolitan* has used Karsner as its special "relationship repair kit" for troubled couples. She was featured in the "Great Book" documentary series on the **Learning Channel** about romance since Jane Austen, narrated by Donald

Sutherland. Heard around the world on *Voice of America*, Karsner was named Innovative Businessperson of the Year by the McLean, Virginia, Chamber of Commerce.

Karsner has a B.A. in Communications from Towson University and received her training from Coach University. She is a Certified Seminar Leader as well as a Master LifePartnerQuest Coach.

Leslie Karsner works as a Romance Coach in Falls Church, Virginia, and travels extensively for speaking engagements. If there is frequent business travel in your organization, you can book her to speak at your next event by calling (703) 241-8099.